History of America
The Struggles of a New Nation
1840 to 1890

Sally Senzell Isaacs

First published in Great Britain by Heinemann Library,
Halley Court, Jordan Hill, Oxford OX2 8EJ,
a division of Reed Educational and Professional Publishing Ltd.
Heinemann is a registered trademark of Reed Educational & Professional
Publishing Limited.

OXFORD MELBOURNE AUCKLAND
JOHANNESBURG BLANTYRE GABORONE
IBADAN PORTSMOUTH NH (USA) CHICAGO

HISTORY OF AMERICA: THE STRUGGLES OF A NEW NATION
was produced for Heinemann Library by Bender Richardson White.

Editor: Lionel Bender
Designer: Ben White
Assistant Editor: Michael March
Picture Researcher: Pembroke Herbert and Nancy Carter
Media Conversion and Typesetting: MW Graphics
Production Controller: Kim Richardson

03 02 01 00 99
10 9 8 7 6 5 4 3 2 1

Printed in Hong Kong

British Library Cataloguing-in-Publication Data.
Isaacs, Sally Senzell
  The struggles of a new nation, 1840–90. - (History of America)
  1. United States - History - 1865–1898 - Juvenile literature
  2. United States - History - 1849–1877 - Juvenile literature
  I. Title.
  973.8

ISBN 0431 05623 4 Hb   ISBN 0431 05635 8 Pb

Acknowledgements
The producers of this book would like to thank the following for permission to
reproduce photographs:
Picture Research Consultants, Mass: pages 6 (National Collection Fine Arts,
Washington D.C.), 8 (National Parks Service), 10 (Library of Congress),
14 (Library of Congress), 16 (Denver Public Library, Western History
Department), 17 (Library of Congress), 19 (Ringling Bros. and Barnum & Bailey
Circus/State Historical Society of Wisconsin), 22t, 24 (Library of Congress), 25
(National Archive), 28 (Library of Congress), 31t (Smithsonian Institute), 32 (From
the Erwin E. Smith Collection of Range Life/Library of Congress), 38 (Archives
and Manuscripts Division of the Oklahoma Historical Society), 40t, 40b (Library
of Congress). Peter Newark's American Pictures: pages 9, 11, 13t, 13b, 15, 18,
20, 21, 26, 27, 29, 31b, 33, 34, 35, 37t, 37b, 39. North Wind Pictures: 23b.

Illustrations by: John James on pages 8/9, 12/13, 14/15, 16/17, 18/19,
24/25, 34/35, 36/37, 38/39, 40/41; Mark Bergin on pages 6/7, 22/23,
28/29, 30/31; Gerald Wood on pages 10/11, 20/21, 26/27, 32/33.
All maps by Stefan Chabluk.

Cover design and make-up by Pelican Graphics. Cover artwork by John James.
Cover photos reproduced with the permission of: Top: Peter Newark's American
Pictures. Centre: Picture Research Consultants (Library of Congress). Bottom:
Picture Research Consultants.

Every effort has been made to contact copyright holders of any material
reproduced in this book. Omissions will be rectified in subsequent printings if
notice is given to the publisher.

Special thanks to Mike Carpenter, Scott Westerfield and Tristan Boyer at
Heinemann Library for editorial and design guidance and direction.

For more information about Heinemann Library books, or to order, please phone
01865 888066, or send a fax to 01865 314091. You can visit our web site at
www.heinemann.co.uk

Any words appearing in the text in bold, **like this**, are
explained in the Glossary.

Major quotations used in this book come from the
following sources. Some of the quotations have been
abridged for clarity.

Page 8: Quote from *Army and Navy Journal* from William
Tecumseh Sherman and the *Settlement of the West* by
Robert G. Athearn. Norman, OK: University of Oklahoma
Press, 1956, page 219.

Page 10: Charles Eastman quote from *The Santee Sioux
Indians* by Terrance Dolan. Broomall, PA: Chelsea House
Publisher, 1997, page 33.

Page 16: Red Cloud quote from *500 Nations* by Alvin M.
Josephy, Jr. New York: Alfred A. Knopf, Inc., 1994, page
389.

Pages 20 and 28: Sitting Bull quotes from *Sitting Bull and
the Battle of the Little Bighorn* by Sheila Black. New
Jersey: Silver Burdett Press, 1989, pages 80 and 115–6.

Page 22: Crazy Horse quote from *Native American
Testimony* by Peter Nabokov. New York: Thomas Y.
Crowell, 1978, page 226.

Page 22: Blackfoot chief quote from *Sitting Bull and the
Battle of the Little Bighorn* by Sheila Black. New Jersey:
Silver Burdett Press, 1989, page 94.

Page 22: Sitting Bull quote from *The Vanishing Race* by
Joseph Dixon. New York: Doubleday, 1913, pages 174–5.

Pages 24 and 25: Chief Joseph quotes from *500 Nations*
by Alvin M. Josephy, Jr. New York: Alfred A. Knopf, Inc.,
1994, pages 413 and 416.

Page 31: Thomas H. Tibbles quote from *500 Nations* by
Alvin M. Josephy, Jr. New York: Alfred A. Knopf, Inc.,
1994, page 441.

Page 38: Hamilton S. Wicks quote from *Eyewitness to
America* by David Colbert. New York: Pantheon Books,
1997, page 289.

The Consultants
Special thanks to Diane Smolinski, Nancy Cope
and Christopher Gibb for their help in the
preparation of this book.

CONTENTS

History of America is a series of nine books arranged chronologically, meaning that events are described in the order in which they happened. However, each book focuses on an important person in American history, so the timespans of the titles overlap. In each book, most articles deal with a particular event or part of American history. Others deal with aspects of everyday life, such as trade, houses, clothing and farming. These general articles cover longer periods of time. The little illustrations at the top left of each article are a symbol of the times. They are identified on page 3.

▼ About the map

This map shows the United States today. It shows the boundaries and names of all the states. Refer to this map, or to the one on pages 42–43, to locate places talked about in this book.

About this book

This book is about America from 1840 to 1890. The term America means 'the United States of America', also called the US. Some historians refer to the native people of America as Amerinds or Indians, as Christopher Columbus did. Others call them Native Americans, as we do. This book focuses on the group of Native Americans called the Sioux. They lived on the Great Plains, along with other Native American groups. The name 'Sioux' was first used by early French explorers. Words in **bold** are described in more detail in the Glossary on page 46.

INTRODUCTION

Americans saw many changes in the 50 years between 1840 and 1890. The population grew by nearly 46 million people. In 1842, a trip across the continent took six months by wagon. After 1869, people could ride a train from coast to coast in 10 days or less. After the **Civil War** ended in 1865, nearly four million African Americans **slaves** started new lives as free Americans. By 1890, more than 14 million **immigrants** had moved to America from all over the world.

This book focuses on one of America's saddest stories, the story of Native Americans. Before Christopher Columbus arrived from Europe in 1492, millions of Native Americans lived throughout the continent. As European **settlers** filled America, the Native Americans were pushed further west. Many died in battles over land, and by starvation and diseases brought by the settlers. Their customs and traditions all but disappeared.

The Sioux people of the **Great Plains** occupied more land than any other Native American group. There were three large groups of Sioux. Sitting Bull belonged to the largest group, the Lakota (sometimes they were called the Teton). The other groups were the Yankton and the Santee. Sitting Bull was one of the most respected holy men and leaders of the Sioux. He tried very hard to keep his people's land and independence. Many of the events in the book took place during Sitting Bull's life. Other events happened after he died. On pages that describe events during his life, there are yellow boxes that tell you what he was doing at the time.

PERMANENT INDIAN COUNTRY

Sitting Bull was born in the wide open land that we now call South Dakota. In 1840, very few white Americans ever saw this land. Many called it Permanent Indian Country. It was rocky and hilly. With its winter blizzards and blazing summer heat, this land seemed worthless to American settlers.

Sitting Bull's people were called Hunkpapa Sioux. They were one of many Native American groups living on the **Great Plains.** Till then, the Sioux had been luckier than Native Americans living in the eastern part of the country. In 1830, the United States government forced nearly 100 **tribes** out of their eastern homeland and moved them to land set aside in present-day Oklahoma. The Native Americans were moved to make room for American **settlers.**

Sioux land was vast and beautiful. The blue sky and rolling grass seemed to go on for ever. Buffalo herds roamed the land. The Sioux hunted the buffalo. They used the meat for food. They used the skins to make clothing and **teepees.** The Sioux believed their god, Wakan Tanka, meaning Great Spirit, was part of everything in nature. The people lived their lives – hunting, preparing food, making homes, even painting their faces – to please the Great Spirit.

▲ Sitting Bull became a medicine man. The Sioux believed that the Great Spirit sent messages through dreams. The medicine man explained dreams. He also helped cure the sick.

► The Mandan were another group of Native Americans living in western Dakota. George Catlin, an American artist, was interested in the lives of Native Americans. In the mid-1800s, he travelled the country painting pictures of them. This is a painting of a Mandan man in a ceremonial dance called the Bull Dance.

A boy named Slow

It was Sioux custom to name a child twice. The first was a childhood name. Later, a person earned an adult name. In 1831, a baby boy was born to a Sioux warrior and his wife. As the child grew, he seemed to spend more time thinking than doing. His parents named him Slow. One day, when Slow was 14 years old, he joined a group of Sioux warriors to attack an enemy tribe. He fought bravely and became a hero. His father proudly gave him a new name that stood for strength and wisdom: Sitting Bull.

▲ The land between the Mississippi River and the Rocky Mountains is called the Great Plains. Many tribes of Native Americans lived on this land.

◀▼ When he was 14, Sitting Bull took part in a traditional Sioux ceremony. The adults built a rounded house of willow rods covered with buffalo skins. It was called a sweat lodge. Inside, they put stones heated by a fire. Then they poured water on the stones to make steam. For a long time, the young boy prayed. Then he was taken to a lonely spot to wait for visions from the Great Spirit to come into his head.

SETTLERS PASSING THROUGH

In 1840, there were more than 17 million American citizens. Each year, more people arrived from Europe and Asia. Most Americans lived in towns or on farms in the East. This part of the continent was becoming crowded. People wanted to spread out.

There was a great deal of land in the West in Oregon Country and California. In 1842, adventurous Americans began heading west on the Oregon Trail and other trails. The 3220-km-long journey crossed **prairies**, deserts and mountains. They also passed through 'Permanent Indian Country'

The United States government built forts along the trail. Soldiers manned the forts to provide supplies for the **settlers** and protect them from Native Americans. The government wanted the cooperation of the Native Americans. They would get it any way possible. The *Army and Navy Journal* described the government's approach to meeting Native Americans. "One of our hands holds the rifle and the other the **peace-pipe**."

▲ A view of Fort Laramie in Wyoming. In 1851, the US government invited the chiefs of many **Great Plains tribes** to the fort to sign a peace **treaty**.

Gold Rush devastation
In 1848, gold was discovered in California. Thousands of people rushed out west in the hope of striking it rich. In doing so, they devastated California's Native American population – between 1848 and 1850, 100,000 died. Some white miners and settlers kidnapped Native Americans and sold them as **slaves.** They shot Native Americans for no valid reason.

▶ Many forts had trading posts where travellers could get supplies. Each spring, thousands of people travelled west on **wagon trains** for protection and companionship. From 1840 to 1860, more than 300,000 people made the journey from Missouri to Oregon or California.

◀ This painting of about 1850 by Charles Wimar shows Native Americans attacking a wagon train. It was clear that the Native Americans' land was no longer their own.

▼ The US government built forts along the westward trails. This fort has a tall fence and watchtower for protection against Native Americans.

Fort Laramie peace treaty
In 1851, many Plains tribes promised the US government not to harm the forts or the settlers on the trails. In exchange, the Native Americans would get $50,000 a year (mostly in food and supplies) for 50 years. Before long, the US **Congress** decided the Native Americans were not worth so much money. They decided to pay $50,000 for only five years.

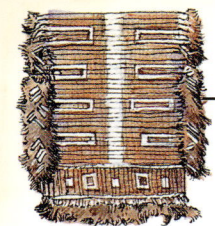

CLAIMING THE LAND

More and more US soldiers moved to the forts to protect the settlers. More and more settlers journeyed through the plains on their way west. The creaking wheels of their wagons frightened the buffalo. Their tin cans and leftover animal bones littered the land.

By 1862, many **settlers** had decided to stay in the **Great Plains**. That year, **Congress** passed the Homestead Act. It promised an area of 65 hectares of land to anyone who would live on the land and farm it.

It seemed impossible for white settlers to share the land with the Native Americans. The two groups viewed the land differently. White settlers wanted to own a piece of land. Native Americans believed a person should not own the earth. A famous Santee Sioux doctor and writer, Charles Eastman, explained: "'To have' was the motto of the white civilization. 'To be' was the motto of the American Indian."

▶ Many settlers built cabins on the land of the Santee Sioux in Minnesota. The Santee lost their hunting grounds. Sometimes angry Santee came to the settlers' cabins to steal food.

▼ This was one of the Sioux **reservations** in present-day South Dakota. A reservation was an area of land set aside for Native Americans. It had an **agency** office from which government workers managed the land.

Chief Sitting Bull
In 1867, Hunkpapa leaders chose Sitting Bull to be their chief. They presented him with a magnificent headdress of eagle feathers.

Chiefs were usually the peacemakers in a tribe. However, they did not make all their decisions alone. Chiefs often asked the advice of elders – members of the tribe who were older and wiser.

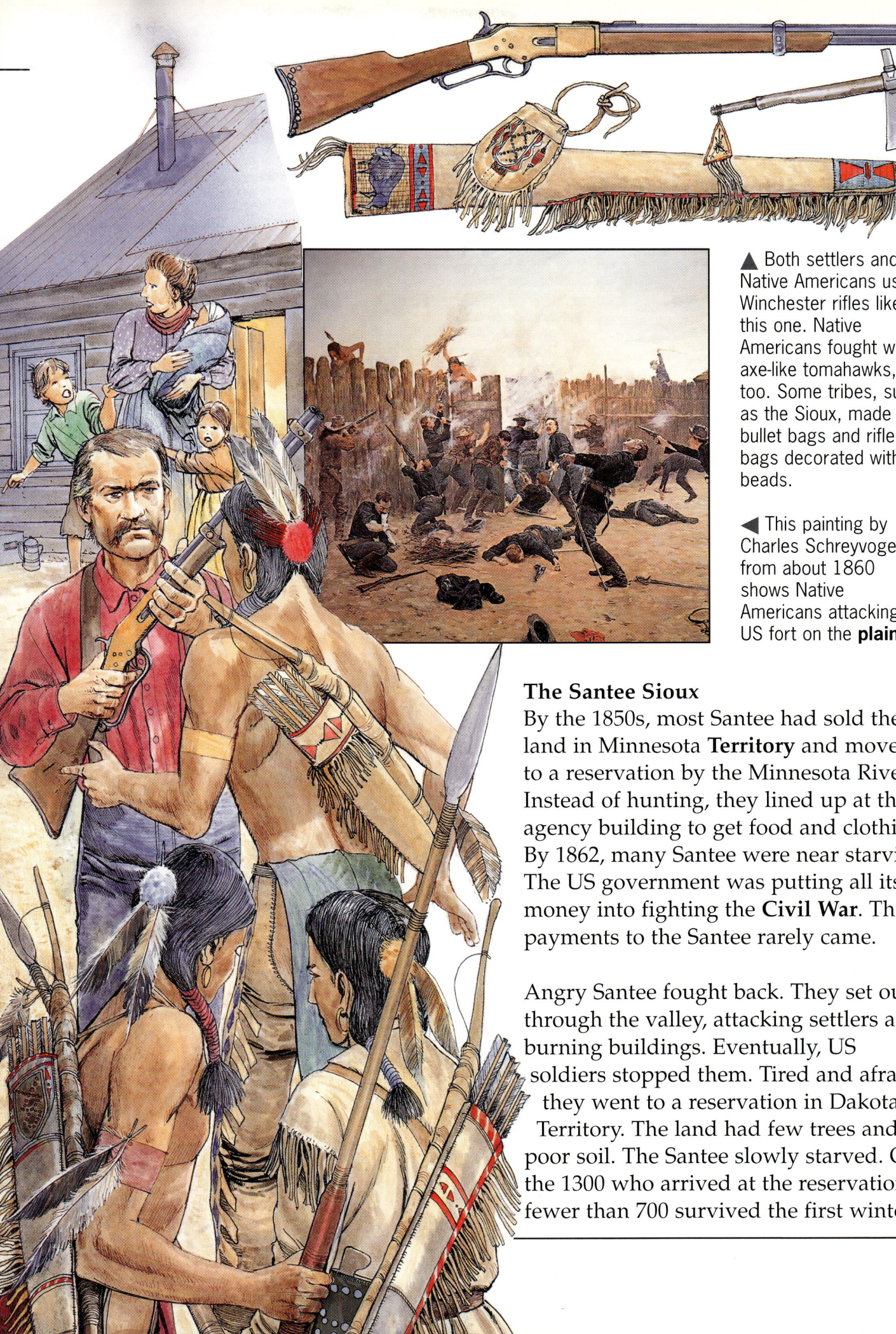

▲ Both settlers and Native Americans used Winchester rifles like this one. Native Americans fought with axe-like tomahawks, too. Some tribes, such as the Sioux, made bullet bags and rifle bags decorated with beads.

◀ This painting by Charles Schreyvogel from about 1860 shows Native Americans attacking a US fort on the **plains**.

The Santee Sioux

By the 1850s, most Santee had sold their land in Minnesota **Territory** and moved to a reservation by the Minnesota River. Instead of hunting, they lined up at the agency building to get food and clothing. By 1862, many Santee were near starving. The US government was putting all its money into fighting the **Civil War**. The payments to the Santee rarely came.

Angry Santee fought back. They set out through the valley, attacking settlers and burning buildings. Eventually, US soldiers stopped them. Tired and afraid, they went to a reservation in Dakota Territory. The land had few trees and poor soil. The Santee slowly starved. Of the 1300 who arrived at the reservation, fewer than 700 survived the first winter.

CATTLE DRIVES

First, white settlers wanted to own the land. Next, they wanted to own the wild animals. Before 1850, five million cattle roamed freely in Texas. Then some Texans gathered large herds of cattle and took them to their ranches. The cattle made these Texans rich.

Several trails led from Texas to railway towns. Some were named after 'trailblazers' – cowboys who set up the routes. (See map on page 42.)

When the **Civil War** ended in 1865, Texas **ranchers** were selling their cattle for $3 or $4 each (about £21 to £28 today). The ranchers knew that people in the East would pay 10 times that price. Easterners loved to eat beef and there were few cattle there. Transportation was the ranchers' greatest problem. The closest railway lines to Texas were about 1930 km away in Kansas and Missouri. Ranchers rounded up their cattle and walked them up to the railways. In 1866, about 260,000 cattle made the long journey.

▼ Longhorn cattle are loaded onto trains in Kansas and taken to such eastern cities as Chicago and St Louis.

▶ James Butler Hickok was in charge of law and order in Abilene. Yet he was a gambler and quick to get into fights, which earned him the name 'Wild Bill Hickok'. He was killed during a card game in Deadwood, Dakota Territory, in 1876.

Dangerous travel

The journey was called a **cattle drive**. It could take up to six months. Some days were hot and dull. Others were cold, wild and dangerous. Cowboys rode beside the herd to keep the cattle together. Occasionally, thunder, a grass fire or gunfire startled the animals, and thousands would take off running. River crossings presented another danger. Cattle sometimes panicked in the water. Often cattle thieves attacked the herd.

Several rugged trails led from Texas to the railways. The trails ended in towns along the railway. They were called cowtowns. Hotels, restaurants and dance halls were built to give the cowboys a well-deserved break before heading back.

Sitting Bull must fight
By 1864, the US Army was trying to move the Sioux out of their hunting grounds by the Powder River in Dakota **Territory**. Sitting Bull ordered his warriors to approach the soldiers with a white flag, a sign of peace. Soldiers fired at the warriors. The warriors attacked until the soldiers retreated. Sitting Bull was proud of his victory, but instead of war he wanted his hunting grounds so that his people would not starve.

▲ This painting by Carl von Iwonski shows the Texas Rangers. There were no police or law officials in these early days. In 1835, several fearless, hard-working Texans organized themselves into the Texas Rangers. They were fast-riding and sharp-shooting. They protected the **settlers** from cattle thieves and bank robbers. They also broke up fights between drunken cowboys and **saloon** keepers. Mostly, they worked without pay.

◀ About 1870, the town of Abilene, Kansas, became a cowtown – the end of the trail for the cattle drives. Cowboys loaded the animals on the trains in Abilene.

▶ Buffalo hunters on the **plains** also got rich, selling hides to make boots and saddles.

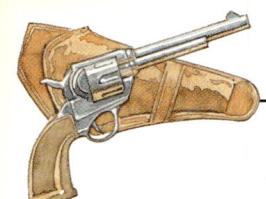

A COWBOY'S LIFE

Everyone thinks of the American cowboy as a tough-fighting, adventure-loving fellow. Real-life cowboys, however, had a tiresome but very important job. For months at a time, they rode across the plains, guiding and protecting thousands of dollars worth of cattle.

About 35,000 cowboys took part in the **cattle drives** out of Texas. Probably about one-third of them were freed African American **slaves** and Mexicans from Texas's southern neighbour. Every spring, they rounded up cattle, sometimes thousands of them, and prepared to hit the trail. First, each animal was **branded** with the owner's initials or other symbol. Then, the pack of cattle and the cowboys – each with a horse to ride and one or two as backups – set out for the railway towns.

▲ **Cowboy equipment**
• saddle – the cowboy's seat for hours each day
• chaps – leather leg protectors
• spurs – boot spikes. A nudge by a spur kept a horse moving quickly.

▲ The cook rode ahead of the others on the chuckwagon. He had a meal ready when the cowboys stopped for the night. Usually they ate beef or bacon and beans.

▶ The round-up on a ranch in Texas – from about 1870.

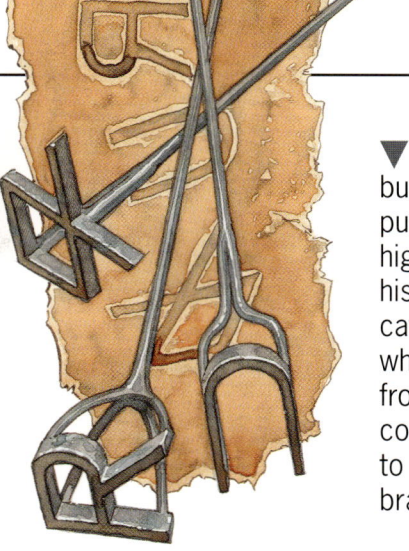

▼ A cowboy sits on his bunk at the ranch to pull on his boots. The high boots protected his legs from the cattles' hoofs and, when on horseback, from their horns. Often, cowboys used **lassos** to bring in calves for branding.

▲ Pony Express riders were also riding the **plains** in 1860 and 1861. They carried mail between St Joseph, Missouri, and Sacramento, California. Artist Frederic Remington painted this scene in 1900.

▲ These are tools to brand the cattle for identification. Each ranch had its own symbol.

▼ To brand a calf, a heated branding iron was pressed into the animal's hide.

Life on the trail

The 'trail boss' rode ahead of the others, looking for good river crossings and signs of danger. Sometimes, Native Americans demanded payment for crossing their land. Occasionally, cattle thieves appeared. On the trail, the cattle ambled in a wide V-shape formation. 'Swing' riders rode beside the herd. 'Drag' riders followed the herd.

Settling down for the night

At dusk, the cattle lay down for the night. The tired cowboys ate their supper and rolled into their blankets. Several stayed awake to guard the cattle. They sang or whistled softly, for their own pleasure and to keep the cattle calm. Cowboys earned about $1 a day – £7 a day at today's value. Other workers in the US earned twice as much.

IMPOSSIBLE PEACE

Ranches, railroads and wagon roads were enclosing the land of the Native Americans. Red Cloud, a chief of the Oglala Sioux tribe, exclaimed: "The white men have crowded the Indians back year by year until we are forced to live in a small country . . . . "

Across the country
1861–1865 Northern and southern states fight a **Civil War**
1865 13th **Amendment** ends slavery
1865 President Abraham Lincoln is shot dead
1867 The United States buys Alaska from Russia
1869 Transcontinental railway connects eastern and western states.

Peace seemed impossible. The US Army built forts on Native American land. The Native Americans attacked the forts. The soldiers then attacked every Native American they saw.

In May 1868, the army invited several tribal chiefs to Fort Laramie. The chiefs signed a **treaty** that seemed encouraging at first. The Sioux could keep their land and hunting grounds in the Black Hills of Dakota **Territory.** It would be called the 'Great Sioux **Reservation'.** US **agents** would work there, but white **settlers** were not allowed. In exchange, all fighting would stop.

Many chiefs, including Red Cloud, liked the treaty. The power of the white people was too great to ask for anything more. Sitting Bull did not approve of the treaty. After all, the government had broken its promises made at Fort Laramie in 1851.

▲ This photograph of Cheyenne and Arapaho chiefs with US soldiers was taken on 28 September 1864. Chief Black Kettle is seated in the middle. Eight weeks after this peacemaking meeting, US soldiers attacked the Native Americans' camp at Sand Creek.

▶ Sitting Bull lived with his people in the Black Hills. Here he is shown wearing a headdress. The Hunkpapa Sioux looked to Sitting Bull for advice. Sitting Bull and Crazy Horse agreed never to start a war with the American soldiers but to fight back to keep their land.

◀ Red Cloud was an Oglala Sioux chief. In 1866, US soldiers began building forts on the Bozeman Trail through his people's hunting grounds on the Powder River in Montana. Red Cloud fought back and won.

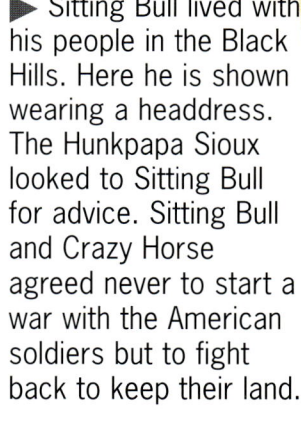

◀ Black Kettle was a Cheyenne chief. He trusted the American soldiers, but paid a terrible price for it. In 1868, US soldiers again attacked his camp at Washita River. This time, they killed him and 100 other Cheyenne.

Broken promises

By 1870, white settlers were building railways just north of the Great Sioux Reservation. Settlers would soon follow. Sitting Bull became friends with the Oglala chief, Crazy Horse. Both men wanted to keep their people's land. They wondered how much longer they could.

◄ This is a photograph of Red Hawk, a Sioux chief. He helped Crazy Horse and Sitting Bull defend the Sioux's last hunting grounds.

17

THE RAILWAY TOWN

When Native Americans saw a train speeding through their hunting grounds, they called it an 'iron horse'. The railway meant progress for American settlers. It meant death for the Native Americans. Buffaloes and iron horses could not live together on the plains.

Railroad workers laid tracks across the buffalo paths. Hired hunters killed thousands of buffaloes to feed the railroad workers. More hunters rode in trains and shot buffaloes. They shipped the skins to the East and left the bodies to rot. In 1870, there were 13 million buffaloes in the West. By 1880, only a few hundred were left. Native Americans were losing their source of food, clothing and shelter. As Native Americans began to starve, more and more of them agreed to move to **reservations**.

▲ ▶ Some Native Americans on reservations lived in **teepees**. Others built wooden cabins to live in. Many of them became farmers, but some depended on the government for food, as in the photograph on the right, which shows cattle being distributed. Sometimes dishonest government workers made Native Americans pay extra charges for their food.

▲ P.T. Barnum started his circus in 1871. He loaded elephants, horses, acrobats and clowns into railway cars and travelled from town to town. In the 1880s, he made James A. Bailey a partner and set up a circus he called 'The Greatest Show on Earth'. This is an advertisement for a joint circus with the Ringling Brothers.

Americans moving faster

By 1869, Americans could travel by train from coast to coast. New railway towns sprang up along the tracks. The railway companies posted ads in the East and in Europe to encourage new **settlers** to move to the **plains**. More settlers meant more railway business in transporting people and goods to the plains.

Many people wondered if crops could grow in dry places such as Kansas, Nebraska, Colorado and South Dakota. The railway companies replied, "Oh, the weather on the plains is changing. Farm machines, **telegraph** wires and the noise of locomotives produce rain." Of course, this was not true. But many thousands of settlers came, nonetheless.

▲ There was great excitement in a town when a train arrived. Trains brought new settlers and visitors. They also brought new clothes and other products for the shops to sell. Best of all, trains brought newspapers and mail – a link to the rest of the world. By 1875, more than 128,000 km of railway lines linked American cities.

HOMELAND IN THE BLACK HILLS

To most Americans, the Black Hills of South Dakota were a vast, worthless wilderness. To Sitting Bull and his Sioux people, the Black Hills were 'Paha Sapa', holy lands. The Fort Laramie Treaty of 1868 promised the Sioux that they could keep the Black Hills "as long as the grass shall grow and the waters flow".

Preparing for battle

In June 1875, hundreds of Sioux and Cheyenne gathered at Sitting Bull's camp. Sitting Bull led meetings with the warriors. He spoke to them: "We are an island of Indians in a lake of whites. We must stand together...." In private, Sitting Bull prayed to the Great Spirit for help.

In the summer of 1874, the Sioux were no longer alone in the Black Hills. George Custer, a fearless lieutenant colonel in the US Army, led 1000 soldiers into the Black Hills. They were looking for a site for a new fort. The fort would guard the workers who were coming to build the railway.

In September, Sitting Bull received a message. The US government wanted to buy the Black Hills to mine gold that had just been found there. Sitting Bull replied, "I do not wish to sell any land to the government."

The only solution is war

The US government would not give up so easily. In December, it issued an order. By 31 January 1876, all Native Americans living in the land of the Great Sioux **Reservation** and the Black Hills must report to their reservation **agencies**. If they did not come freely, they would be taken by force.

Sitting Bull knew he could not lead his people to the agency. It would mean travelling 400 km during the harsh winter. His people would not survive the journey. He knew it was time for war.

▶ To contact the Great Spirit, Sitting Bull went to the special Sioux ceremony called the Sun Dance.

A pole made from the sacred cottonwood tree was erected. Sitting Bull pierced his skin with sharp hooks, or skewers. These skewers were attached by ropes to the pole. As ceremonial drums beat, Sitting Bull danced around a pole.

The purpose of the dance was to cause pain to the dancer. Then the Great Spirit would speak to him. Sitting Bull danced for three days. Then the Great Spirit sent him a dream: His people would defeat their white enemy.

▼ In 1875, a group of Sioux leaders went to Washington DC, to complain about their treatment on the reservations.

▼ Sioux scouts watch as Custer marches his blue-coated soldiers into the Black Hills. For now, the soldiers are looking for a site to build a fort. They will soon return to cause more problems for the Sioux. These green valleys and majestic mountains have been homeland to the Sioux for hundreds of years.

▲ This painting by Charles Schreyvogel shows General Custer demanding that Native Americans return to their reservation.

◄ 'General' George A. Custer never gave up a fight. Native Americans called him 'Long Hair'. He was a lieutenant colonel, but for a time was a major general during the **Civil War**.

▼ In July 1874, Custer's men found a nugget of gold in the Black Hills. By spring 1875, 1000 miners were camping **illegally** in the Sioux homeland. This angered Sitting Bull and Crazy Horse.

BATTLE AT LITTLE BIGHORN

In June 1876, Sitting Bull and Crazy Horse moved their people to a place they called Greasy Grass. It was near the Little Bighorn River in present-day Montana. Crazy Horse later said, "All we wanted was peace and to be left alone." The US Army had other plans.

Up to 15,000 Sioux, Cheyenne and Arapaho came to live at the camp with Crazy Horse and Sitting Bull. They wanted to keep their land at any price. Sitting Bull said, "We are here to protect our wives and children, and we must not let the soldiers get to them."

On 25 June 1876 Lieutenant Colonel Custer led 650 soldiers to the Little Bighorn Valley. With 265 soldiers, he charged into Sitting Bull and Crazy Horse's camp. Crazy Horse led his warriors in defence. They outnumbered the soldiers ten to one. The air filled with gunshots and arrows. When the dust settled, Custer and his men were dead.

▶ The rest of Custer's troops, led by Major Marcus Reno and Captain Frederick Benteen, fought warriors, including Sitting Bull, on nearby hillsides. The warriors were winning, but more soldiers were on the way. Sitting Bull decided it was time to lead his people out of Little Bighorn Valley.

US Army versus Native Americans
Some conflicts lasted several years, with an attack here and a massacre there. Sometimes Native Americans were victorious. Sometimes they left their land to the settlers. These are some of the last battles.

1846–1864 Navajo conflicts in Arizona
1854–1890 Sioux Wars on the **Great Plains**
1861–1890 Apache conflicts in Arizona, New Mexico, Texas
1864 Sand Creek Massacre in Colorado

1872–1873 Moduc War in California and Oregon
1876 Battle at Little Bighorn in Montana
1877 Nez Perce War at White Bird Canyon in Montana
1879 Meeker Massacres in Colorado

◀ During the Sun Dance, Sitting Bull dreamed of victory over the soldiers. His dream came true. This is a drawing by Red Horse of the Lakota **tribe.** He shows the Native American's victory over Custer. The soldiers fought with rifles and swords, the Native Americans with guns, rifles, bows and arrows, shields, tomahawks and knives.

Sitting Bull leaves

News of Custer's defeat spread through America. Hundreds of soldiers poured into Sioux country to put an end to the Native Americans. Sitting Bull and Crazy Horse led their people in different directions. Crazy Horse went to the Black Hills. Sitting Bull went towards the Yellowstone River. Both groups dodged soldiers along the way.

In October, Sitting Bull received hopeless news. President Ulysses Grant was forcing all chiefs to give up their land in the Black Hills and the Powder River Valley. America offered no place to live, except the **reservations**. Sitting Bull led his people into Canada. Though the weather was cold and the buffalo did not roam there, perhaps his people could live in freedom in Canada.

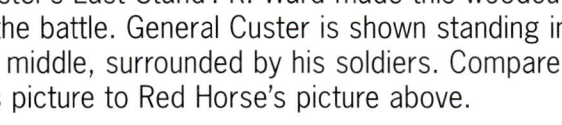

◀ Americans called the Battle of Little Bighorn 'Custer's Last Stand'. R. Ward made this woodcut of the battle. General Custer is shown standing in the middle, surrounded by his soldiers. Compare this picture to Red Horse's picture above.

"I Am Tired Of Fighting"

"You might as well expect the rivers to run backward as that any man who was born free should be contented penned up and denied liberty to go where he pleases," said Chief Joseph of the Nez Perce people. They, too, were losing their land.

The Nez Perce lived west of the Sioux land, where Oregon, Washington and Idaho now meet. For many years, they were friendly with white **settlers** who travelled through their land. But in 1860, miners discovered gold there. In 1863, many Nez Perce sold their land and moved to an Idaho **reservation.** Chief Joseph and about 250 others would not go.

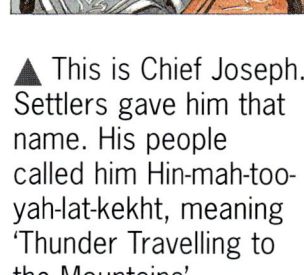

▲ This is Chief Joseph. Settlers gave him that name. His people called him Hin-mah-too-yah-lat-kekht, meaning 'Thunder Travelling to the Mountains'.

▼ The Apache were the last Native American group to give up. They lived in the south-western part of the US. In 1886, the army finally caught up with them. This is a photograph of their leader, Geronimo (right) and three braves. The Apache moved to a reservation.

The Sioux were trying to keep their people alive on the Dakota reservation. Many Native Americans died of hunger and disease. Others died of misery and sadness. This burial platform was a common sight. The Sioux placed a body on a platform, closer to the Great Spirit, until the ground thawed enough to bury it.

No escape

In 1876, government officials insisted that Chief Joseph move his 250 people to the reservation. First, one settler attacked a Nez Perce. Then, several soldiers and Native Americans fired at each other. Chief Joseph realized that soldiers would soon outnumber his people. He gathered them – mostly children and old people – and headed through the mountains to Canada. He hoped to join forces with Sitting Bull's people, who had fled there.

US soldiers attacked the Nez Perce all along the way. Finally, on 5 October 1877, Chief Joseph **surrendered.** He was less than 65 km from Canada, but could take no more. He said, "The little children are freezing to death. Some of [my people] have run away to the hills, and have no blankets, no food. I am tired of fighting. My heart is sick and sad. From where the sun now stands I will fight no more forever."

The government promised to return the Nez Perce to the Idaho reservation. Instead, they were taken to a disease-ridden reservation in Oklahoma. By 1885, only 150 Nez Perce were alive.

The Nez Perce tried to escape to Canada. The journey was 1600 km. On the way, they passed through Yellowstone National Park. They captured sightseers, but then let them go. One army unit after another chased the Nez Perce. Eventually, they surrendered.

Sitting Bull's 187 people were starving in Canada. In July 1881, he brought them back to the United States to surrender. At the border, Sitting Bull was arrested for Custer's murder. He was taken as prisoner to Fort Randall in South Dakota. This is a photograph of Sitting Bull and his family at the fort.

AMERICA'S 100TH BIRTHDAY

While Americans in the West worried about land, Americans in the East were celebrating. In 1876, the United States was 100 years old. The birthday party was held in Philadelphia, where America's founders signed the Declaration of Independence in 1776.

The party was called the Centennial Exposition. Centennial means 100th anniversary. An exposition is a show or exhibition. This show lasted from May to November. Citizens from more than 35 countries showed off their best paintings, foods and inventions. Americans were proudest of all.

For all the world to see
There were over 200 buildings at the exposition. The Main Hall was called the world's largest building. It covered 14.2 hectares. There were also glass buildings and many large statues. George Washington's coat and vest were on display. So was Ben Franklin's printing press. There was a copy of the Liberty Bell made of tobacco. A copy of the dome of the Capitol building in Washington DC was made of apples.

More than 10 million people came to see the new inventions. There was a sewing machine, a washing machine and a typewriter which would speed up the time-consuming work of writing letters.

▲ This photograph from 1884 of the East River piers in New York City was taken from the newly opened Brooklyn Bridge. At the time, Americans hailed this iron bridge with steel cables as 'the eighth wonder of the world'. By 1880, workers could turn iron into steel inexpensively. Steel was stronger than iron. People began to use steel to build machinery, railways and buildings.

▼ A view of the Centennial Exposition halls in Philadelphia.

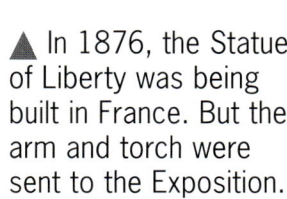

▲ In 1876, the Statue of Liberty was being built in France. But the arm and torch were sent to the Exposition.

By 1871, Chicago was a big city. Downtown Chicago had hundreds of buildings – almost all built of wood. In October 1871, a fire blazed through these buildings. It lasted for 24 hours, killing at least 300 people and destroying $200 million in property.

Bell's invention

At the Exposition, everyone was talking about Alexander Graham Bell's invention called the telephone. Just two months before the Centennial, he found a way to make sound waves from his voice travel over a wire. A reporter from the *New York Tribune* wondered, "Of what use is such an invention?"

In the Machinery Hall was George Corliss's steam engine, the world's largest machine. President Grant started up the engine. Steam from the engine turned wheels that pulled belts strung overhead. The belts made 8000 smaller machines work.

▲ In 1877, Thomas Edison, of New Jersey, made a phonograph. This recorded and played back sound.

▲ In 1879, Edison invented the electric light bulb. Since 1876, there had been over 14,000 new inventions.

THE WILD WEST SHOW

The fighting between Native Americans and US soldiers was a very serious matter. But one man turned it into entertainment. In 1883, William Cody started Buffalo Bill's Wild West Show. The travelling show entertained people throughout the country.

Millions of Americans knew the name Buffalo Bill Cody. He brought the Wild West right into their home towns. People who had never travelled west of the Mississippi River loved Bill's exciting shows. They watched sharpshooters, rodeo riders and high-kicking dancers. According to Bill's show, western America was full of excitement.

Sitting Bull joins the show

In 1885, Bill Cody went to Dakota **Territory.** By now, Sitting Bull had been released from Fort Randall and was living at Standing Rock **Reservation.** Bill asked Sitting Bull to join his show. He would add an act about the Battle at Little Bighorn. Sitting Bull, who had been arguing about supplies with the **agent** of the reservation, agreed to join the show.

Now, the Wild West Show was more popular than ever. Each night, silence fell through the crowd. Then gunfire cracked the silence, and Sitting Bull rode out on a grey circus horse. The crowd exploded with cheers. They loved seeing a real-life Native American. Sitting Bull travelled to several US cities. As the show was about to go to Europe, he decided to return to the reservation. He knew his people needed him.

Sitting Bull sees America

While travelling with the Wild West Show, Sitting Bull saw a different side of America. He saw busy streets, bustling carriages, tall buildings and huge ships. He also saw the sad faces of poor, hungry people. He once said, "The white man knows how to make everything, but he does not know how to distribute it." Sitting Bull gave most of the money he earned to poor children.

▼ Annie Oakley was part of Buffalo Bill's Wild West Show. Her nickname was Little Sure Shot. She could shoot a hole through a playing card tossed 27 m away. Annie toured the United States and Europe with the show. During World War I (1914–1918), she gave shooting lessons to American soldiers.

Photographers were interested in the Native Americans of the West. They wanted to record Native American ways of life before they died out. In 1886, C.S. Fly went to Tombstone, Arizona, to photograph the Apache.

▼ Sitting Bull parades at a Wild West Show.

▲ America was now buzzing with activity. Towns in the North such as Pittsburgh, Pennsylvania, were filled with factories and steel mills. Telephone poles and electric power plants were going up in every city.

◄ Bullalo Bill's Wild West Show poster.

▼ From 1868 to 1872, William Cody lived in the West. He led groups of white buffalo hunters on the **plains.** He also was a scout who helped the army find Native Americans. 'Buffalo Bill' Cody liked being famous and decided to start his own Wild West Show in 1883.

DEATH OF A DREAM

By 1887, there were no more free Native Americans. They all lived on reservations run by the US government. The white man had won North America. Red Cloud, a chief of the Oglala Lakota Sioux, said, "They made us many promises . . . but they kept but one; they promised to take our land and they took it."

The Sioux were miserable on the **reservations**. No longer could they roam, hunt buffalo, rejoice in their religious celebrations. Now, they stood in lines at the **agency** office to pick up poor-quality food and clothing. White teachers tried to teach them to become Christians and banned Sioux ceremonies.

In 1887, the government passed the Dawes Act. This act divided the land on the reservations. Each Sioux family was given a plot of land to farm. But the Sioux were hunters, not farmers. White **settlers** approached the unhappy Sioux and tricked them into selling their land for low prices.

▲ Sitting Bull's death. The government blamed Sitting Bull for the Ghost Dances at Standing Rock, his reservation. On 15 December 1890, Lakota police came to arrest him, as shown above. Sitting Bull's friends gathered. Both sides fired rifles. Sitting Bull was accidentally struck by a bullet fired from his people. The great chief died instantly.

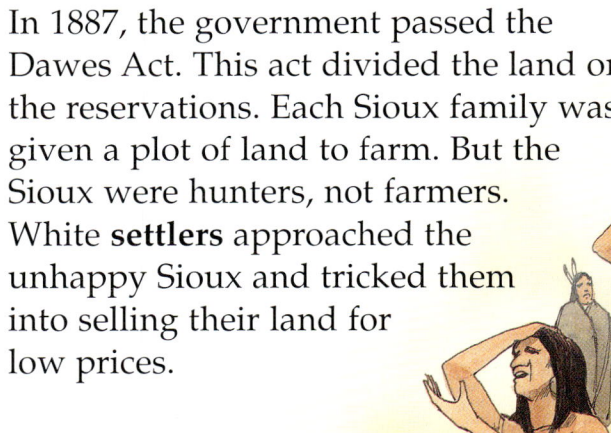

▶ The saddened **Great Plains** people began to practise a new, peaceful religion. They stood in a circle and chanted special prayers. They danced for days. As they became exhausted, they saw visions of their joyful past. White soldiers were afraid of this ceremony. They called it a Ghost Dance.

▶ Ghost dancers believed a shirt like this would protect them against the soldiers' bullets.

The final shots

After Sitting Bull's death, 350 of his people headed towards Pine Creek Sioux reservation in South Dakota. As they neared Wounded Knee Creek on 28 December 1890, soldiers surrounded them and demanded their guns.

No one is sure whether the first shot came from a Sioux or soldier. But other shots followed. The Sioux ran. The soldiers fired at anything that moved. It is estimated that only 50 Sioux survived the Battle of Wounded Knee. Hundreds of years of fighting between whites and Native Americans had ended.

◀ The soldiers who fought at Wounded Knee were once commanded by General George Custer. The troops stood on a hill overlooking the Native Americans. After hearing the first gunshot, they fired rifles and larger guns, like this one.

▲ Thomas H. Tibbles, a newspaper reporter, saw the Battle at Wounded Knee and wrote: "Though the active attack lasted perhaps 20 minutes, the firing continued for an hour or two." This painting by Frederic Remington in about 1900, shows the aftermath of the battle.

THE CATTLE RANCH

The dwindling population of Native Americans settled for the ugly conditions of the reservations. Meanwhile, Texans and other people in the West and South-west built large ranches. In the 1870s and early 1880s, cattle ranching became big business.

The first **ranchers** did not own any land. They built themselves a shack in the middle of open land. They rounded up the wild cattle that wandered in the area and **claimed** them as their own. As ranchers made more money selling their cattle, they began to build big ranches.

Many cowboys, also called cowhands, worked on a ranch. They rode horses around the land to keep the cattle from wandering away. They also guarded the herd against mountain lions. Cattle thieves were another danger. That is why ranchers **branded** their animals with special symbols.

▶ By the 1880s, there were many large ranches in the South-west. There were different areas on the ranch:
1. ranch house where the ranch-owner lived
2. corral where cowhands gathered the young cattle and branded them
3. bunkhouse where the cowhands slept
4. cookhouse where the cowhands ate
5. bath house where all ranch-workers washed after the day's work
6. cattle on the range.

▶ This photo of about 1890 by Erwin E. Smith shows cattle on the Matador Range in Texas. They are heading from the ranch to the railway in Lubbock, Texas. Cowboys guided the cattle on the journey, a trip that could take several months.

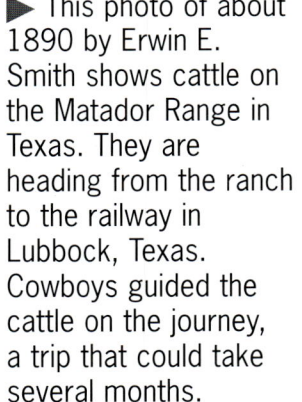

There were many sheep ranchers in the West. Sheep provided valuable wool and meat. But sheep ate the grass until it was too short for cattle to eat. Sheep ranchers used barbed wire fences to keep cattle off their land.

Problems for big ranchers

Around 1886, freezing temperatures hit the South-west. Thousands of cattle froze to death. Then there was a period when little rain fell. Grazing land dried up and more cattle died. Then farmers came west and **claimed** land. They fenced in their land with newly invented barbed wire. Ranchers hated barbed wire. It divided up the open land and blocked their cattle's watering holes.

This is a photograph of Nat Love taken in about 1875. He had been a **slave** in Tennessee. When slaves were freed after the **Civil War,** he went west and became a cowhand. For 20 years, he worked on **cattle drives**, taking cattle from Texas to Kansas and other railway towns.

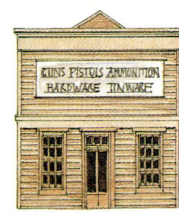
A FRONTIER TOWN

By 1885, western land was dotted with frontier towns. Some towns started as camps where miners pitched their tents. Other towns sprang up when the railway tracks were laid. Places such as Dodge City in Kansas and Tombstone in Arizona became bustling frontier towns.

Towns grew wherever miners, farmers or cowhands gathered. People needed food, clothing, supplies. Before long, shops were built on either side of a dirt road. That became Main Street.

Many shops looked bigger on the outside than they were on the inside. The false fronts with their large signs attracted customers. The dirt roads were dusty in dry weather and muddy in the rain. Shopkeepers built wooden walkways to keep the dirt out of their shops. Customers on horseback tied their horses to hitching posts outside the shops.

About every 10 days, a stagecoach came to town. It brought passengers from other **frontier** towns or travellers who just got off a train from the East. Stagecoaches also brought the mail and other news to the townspeople. Wagons pulled by horses and oxen brought building supplies and food. Streets were made very wide so that the animals could turn wagons around in the road.

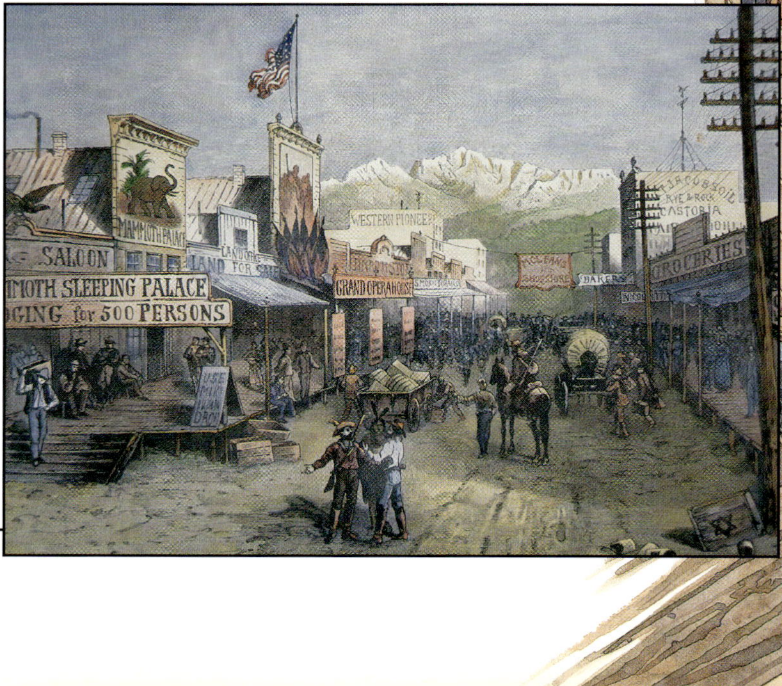

▶ This is a painting of a typical frontier town in the West around 1880. Towns were not only connected by stagecoaches and railways. **Telegraph** wires allowed people to communicate over long distances. By 1875, new advances in the telegraph could send five messages at once over one wire.

34

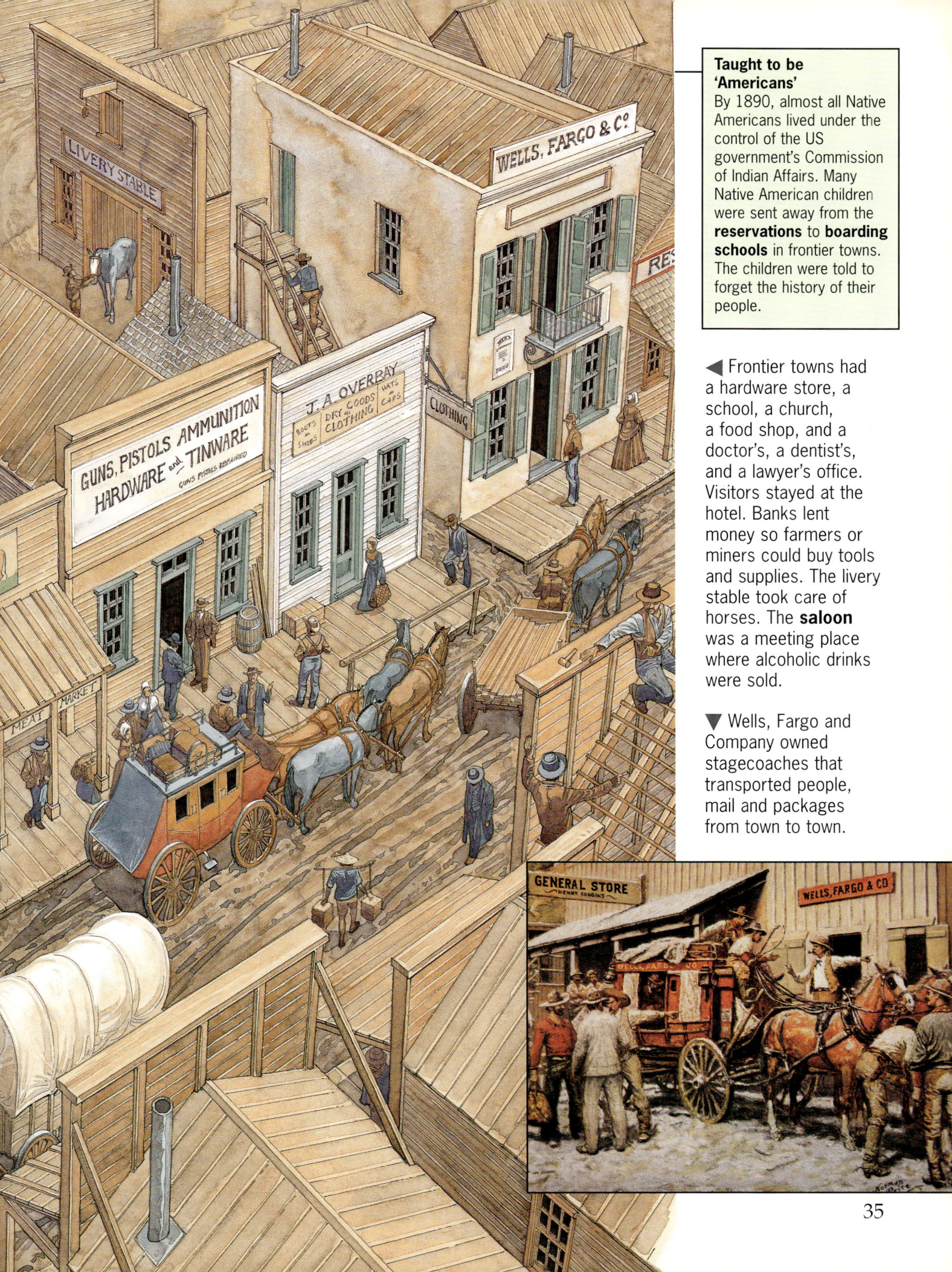

◀ Frontier towns had a hardware store, a school, a church, a food shop, and a doctor's, a dentist's, and a lawyer's office. Visitors stayed at the hotel. Banks lent money so farmers or miners could buy tools and supplies. The livery stable took care of horses. The **saloon** was a meeting place where alcoholic drinks were sold.

▼ Wells, Fargo and Company owned stagecoaches that transported people, mail and packages from town to town.

OUTLAWS AND LAWMEN

Easterners called frontier towns 'The Wild West'. Bank robberies and shoot-outs were common. People took what they thought they deserved. They settled their own problems without police officers or judges. Just two laws were accepted by everyone: you cannot shoot a man in the back or insult a woman.

On 31 January 1874, the Iron Mountain Express chugged into the station at Gads Hills, Missouri. Five men boarded the train and demanded jewellery and money from the passengers. Before riding away, one of the robbers handed the train conductor a note and told him to give it to the newspapers. It was a news article he wanted printed. It described this very robbery. The article ended with: *The James–Younger gang has struck again!*

Combating crime waves

Frank and Jesse James and Cole, Jim and Bob Younger led one of the worst crime waves of the Wild West. They committed the country's first bank robbery in 1866 and the first train robbery in 1872. Local people tried to find ways to deal with outlaws. They formed vigilante groups to search for suspected lawbreakers. Often they killed those that they caught.

▼ This outlaw outside a **saloon** knows he cannot outshoot the **marshall**. He has thrown down his gun and his gang is running away. Local people often served as **deputy** marshalls to help stop outlaws.

▶ Billy the Kid
His real name was Henry McCarty. At age 18, he changed it to William H. Bonney. He lived just 21 years as a cowboy, cattle thief and killer, and was known as Billy the Kid.

▶ Jesse James
(far right) In 1881, Missouri's governor offered $10,000 for Jesse James – dead or alive. One of his 'friends', Robert Ford, shot and killed Jesse on 3 April 1882.

Billy the Kid

Jesse James

◀ This picture shows Billy the Kid shooting a bartender in 1880. It appeared in *Police Gazette*. Some legends say Billy killed 21 men. More likely, he killed about six. In November 1880, Sheriff Pat Garrett of Lincoln County, New Mexico, finally caught Billy. But on 28 April 1881, he escaped from jail. Garrett found him and killed him on July 14.

Law and order

After a state was officially part of the US, suspects were given a trial by **jury.** Officers called marshalls and **sheriffs** tried to keep lawbreakers in line. Some famous lawmen of the day were Wild Bill Hickok, Bat Masterson and Wyatt Earp. Lawmen were supposed to be elected. Sometimes the job went to the first brave volunteer.

▲ Martha Jane Canary earned the nickname Calamity Jane. She said she had been a gold miner, Pony Express rider, sharpshooter, cowhand and nurse.

◀ Pearl Hart was a stagecoach bandit. For her crimes, she once spent time in prison.

THE RUSH FOR LAND

For many years, settlers stayed away from one area of the plains. It was called Indian Territory, and is today in Oklahoma. The US government had promised this land to the Cherokees and other Native American groups. By the 1880s, settlers wanted this land, too.

Posters like this one announced the opening of new land. Settlers hurried out to claim some.

The US government announced that at noon on 22 April 1889, a strip of land in western Oklahoma would be open to **settlers**. People lined up with their horses and wagons. They were eager to set up a tent to **claim** a piece of land. A writer for *Cosmopolitan Magazine*, Hamilton S. Wicks, described his experience there: "Suddenly the air was pierced with the blast of a bugle. (Horses), no longer restrained by the hands that held their bridles, bounded forward into the beautiful land of Oklahoma.... The race was not over when you reached the particular lot.... The contest still was who would erect their little tents soonest."

▼ This photo shows settlers rushing off to claim newly opened land. In the 'land rush', most people rode horses, but some rode bicycles or ran.

▶ By 1890, farming was big business. Farmers invested money to buy steam-powered tractors. They sent their crops by trains to cities in the East. Some crops were sent by ship to Europe. Between 1860 and 1890, more land was turned into farmland than in the previous 250 years.

▶ Before noon on 22 April 1889, the land called Guthrie, Oklahoma, was empty. By sundown, the town had a population of 15,000 people living in tents. The next day, the people elected a mayor and built 500 small wooden houses. In just five months, Guthrie had broad streets, parks, bridges, electric lights, a hotel, three general stores and 50 **saloons.** This photograph was taken in April 1893.

▶ Settlers staked their claim at a government land office and protected their land with rifles.

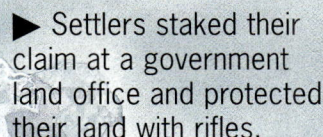

The end of the frontier

Throughout the 1800s, Americans kept moving west to the wilderness and unsettled lands called the **frontier**. By 1890, the United States no longer had a frontier. Settlers occupied almost all of the land, either in cities, farms or towns.

Cowboys and the Wild West were also coming to an end. Railway lines stretched all the way to Texas by 1890. **Cattle drives** were unnecessary. Law and order came to the railway towns in Kansas and Missouri.

Also, America's first settlers, the Native Americans, had nearly vanished. Before European settlers came, there were many millions of Native Americans. By 1890, less than 250,000 survived.

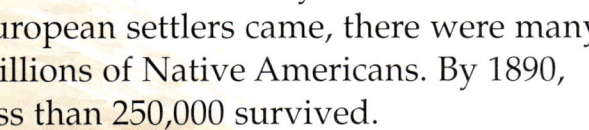

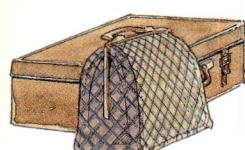

HOPEFUL IMMIGRANTS

By 1890, America's population was 63 million. That was double the population in 1860. Over 14 million of the new people moved to America from Europe. They came for many reasons. Above all, they came with the hope of living a better life.

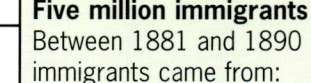

Five million immigrants
Between 1881 and 1890 immigrants came from:
1. Germany 1,452,970
2. England/Scotland/ Wales 807,357
3. Ireland 655,482
4. Norway/Sweden 568,362
5. Canada/Newfoundland 393,304
6. Italy 307,309
7. Russia 213,290
8. Denmark 88,132
9. China 61,711
10. Poland 51,806
11. France 50,464
12. Central and South America 33,663
13. Spain and Portugal 21,397

America promised an opportunity to own land or get a job. More importantly, there was freedom. Many people from Germany, Russia and eastern Europe left their countries because they were being punished for their religious or political beliefs. In some countries, police stormed Jewish neighbourhoods, destroyed property and killed people.

Almost 1.5 million Germans came to America between 1881 and 1890. One out of every ten people in Greece came, too. One-third of the people of Iceland headed for America, along with people from Italy, Ireland, Sweden and China. Most came by ship. Some came by rail from Canada.

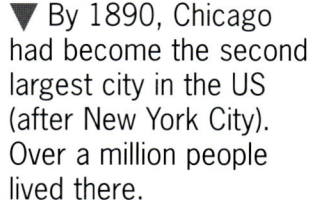
▼ By 1890, Chicago had become the second largest city in the US (after New York City). Over a million people lived there.

► This is Hester Street in lower Manhattan, New York City. By 1900, this area was the most crowded place in the world. Several families lived together in tiny apartments above the shops. They shopped at the outdoor pushcarts. Many Jewish **immigrants** settled in this neighbourhood. During this time, more Jews lived in New York City than in any other city in the world.

▼ Nearly every day a shipload of immigrants arrived in New York City. The journey from countries such as Holland or Italy took about two weeks. Immigrants bought the cheapest one-way tickets, usually $10 or $15 (equivalent to about £120 or £180 today). Immigrants who arrived after 1886 were welcomed into New York Harbour by the Statue of Liberty.

America welcomes newcomers

America's iron, steel and clothing factories needed strong, skilled workers. Immigrants were willing to work for the lowest wages. Railway companies encouraged immigrants to settle in the West – and travel by train to get there.

Immigrants in the cities faced many problems. They arrived with little money. They mostly spoke no English. They had no homes. The lucky ones moved into crowded apartments with relatives. They lived in neighbourhoods called 'Little Italy' and 'Chinatown'. People there spoke their language and shared their customs.

41

Historical Map of America

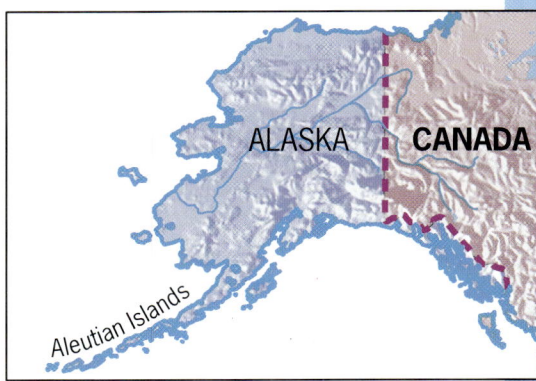

ALASKA   CANADA

Aleutian Islands

On the map

This map shows the United States in 1890. There were 44 states. Until 1889, North and South Dakota were called Dakota **Territory.** The land between the Mississipppi River and the Rocky Mountains is called the **Great Plains**. Once Native Americans lived throughout the continent. By 1890, the United States government forced them off their land and onto **reservations** throughout the Great Plains and West. Before railways reached Texas, cowboys used cattle trails from Texas to Kansas and Missouri. By the 1890s, five railways stretched across the continent.

Kauai

Oahu

Maui

Hawaii

HAWAIIAN ISLANDS

PACIFIC OCEAN

Seattle
WASHINGTON
Columbia
Portland
OREGON
Modoc

ROUTE OF THE NEZ PERCE
Missouri
MONTANA
Nez Perce
Yellowstone
Little Big Horn River
IDAHO
YELLOWSTONE NATIONAL PARK
Shoshone
Snake
Powder

CALIFORNIA TRAIL
CENTRAL PACIFIC RAILROAD
Promontory Point
WYOMING
UNION PACIFIC RAILROAD

PONY EXPRESS TRAIL
Sacramento
San Francisco
NEVADA
UTAH TERRITORY
Colorado
COLORADO

CALIFORNIA
Navajo

Los Angeles
Colorado
Santa Fé
NEW MEXICO TERRITORY
Apache
Rio Grande
Tombstone

R O C K Y   M O U N T A I N S

— River
•••• Overland trail
- - - Cattle trail
⋯⋯ Railway
Native American tribal areas

0   250   500 miles
0   400   800 kilometres

Hudson Bay

C A N A D A

St. Lawrence

NORTH DAKOTA
Missouri
Bismarck

MINNESOTA

Lake Superior

Lake Champlain

MAINE

VERMONT
NEW HAMPSHIRE

Lake Huron

Lake Ontario

NEW YORK

MASSACHUSETTS
Boston
RHODE ISLAND
CONNECTICUT

St. Paul

Crow
Deadwood
Western Sioux
BLACK HILLS
Cheyenne

Eastern Sioux

Minnesota

WISCONSIN

Middle Sioux

SOUTH DAKOTA

THE

Fort Randall
Sioux City

Lake Michigan

Mississippi

IOWA

MICHIGAN

Chicago

Lake Erie

PENNSYLVANIA
Pittsburgh

Delaware
Hudson

New York City
Statue of Liberty
Philadelphia
NEW JERSEY
DELAWARE
WASHINGTON D.C.
MARYLAND

Fort Laramie
NEBRASKA
Omaha
Ogallala
OREGON TRAIL

Missouri

ILLINOIS

INDIANA

OHIO

Gettysburg

GREAT

St. Joseph

Sedalia

Ohio

St. Louis

WEST VIRGINIA

APPALACHIAN MOUNTAINS

VIRGINIA
Richmond
Appomattox

Ute
KANSAS
Dodge City
Abilene

Kansas City

MISSOURI

KENTUCKY

NORTH CAROLINA

PLAINS

Wichita

SEDALIA TRAIL

SHAWNEE TRAIL

Apache
Guthrie

INDIAN TERRITORY

ARKANSAS

TENNESSEE

Mississippi

SOUTH CAROLINA

Charleston

WESTERN TRAIL

CHISOLM TRAIL

Atlanta

ALABAMA

GEORGIA

Savannah

Fort Worth
Dallas

LOUISIANA

MISSISSIPPI

ATLANTIC OCEAN

T E X A S

GOODNIGHT LOVING TRAIL

New Orleans

San Antonio

Houston

FLORIDA

Rio Grande

MEXICO

G U L F   O F   M E X I C O

C U B A

FAMOUS PEOPLE OF THE TIME

P.T. Barnum, 1810–1891, started an entertaining show with a midget named General Tom Thumb, a singer named Jenny Lind and a giant elephant named Jumbo. He helped start a circus that today is called Ringling Brothers and Barnum and Bailey Circus.

Alexander Graham Bell, 1847–1922, was an inventor and teacher of the deaf, best known for inventing the telephone.

Billy the Kid, 1859–1881, was a cattle thief and a killer in New Mexico. He was one of the most famous outlaws in the Wild West.

Black Kettle, 1803?–1868, was a Cheyenne chief. He tried to live peacefully with white settlers, but soldiers attacked his people in Colorado and Oklahoma. He was killed by Custer's troops by the Washita River.

Calamity Jane (Martha Canary), 1852–1903, was a famous woman on the frontier. She was a skilled horsewoman and expert rifle-shooter.

William (Buffalo Bill) Cody, 1846–1917, volunteered to serve in Kansas during the Civil War. He later became a buffalo hunter. He is best known for his Wild West shows.

Crazy Horse, 1844?–1877, was a chief of the Oglala Sioux. He led warriors to victory over Lieutenant Colonel (General) George Custer in the Battle at Little Bighorn.

George A. Custer, 1839–1876, was a Civil War general and later a fighter against Native Americans. He and his soldiers were killed by Sioux and Cheyenne in the Battle at Little Bighorn.

Thomas Edison, 1847–1931, was one of the greatest inventors in history. His work helped bring electric lights, phonographs and motion pictures to the world.

James Garfield, 1831–1881, was the 20th US president. He was assassinated only a few months after taking office.

Geronimo, 1829–1909, was an Apache warrior. After escaping from an Arizona reservation and fighting soldiers and settlers for many years, he surrendered in 1886. He spent the rest of his life in Oklahoma, where he was a celebrity at many fairs.

Ulysses S. Grant, 1822–1885, was commander in chief of the Union army in the Civil War. From 1869–1877, he was the 18th US. president.

IMPORTANT DATES AND EVENTS

THE UNITED STATES from 1840 to 1865
1842 pioneers go west on Oregon Trail
1845 Texas and Florida become states
1846–1848 US–Mexican War
1846 Iowa becomes a state
1848 Oregon becomes part of the US
1848 Wisconsin becomes a state
1848 California gold rush begins
1850 California becomes a state
1851 Fort Laramie Treaty promises Native Americans money and food for land
1858 Minnesota becomes a state
1859 Oregon becomes a state
1860–1861 Pony Express operating
1861 Kansas becomes a state
1861–1865 Civil War in the East
1862 Homestead Act opens Great Plains land to settlers
1862 settlers defeat Santee Sioux in Minnesota
1863 Emancipation Proclamation frees slaves in Confederate states
1863 West Virginia becomes a state
1864 Nevada becomes a state
1865 13th Amendment ends slavery

THE UNITED STATES from 1866 to 1890
1866 Red Cloud's War begins
1867 Nebraska becomes a state
1867 US buys Alaska from Russia
1868 second Fort Laramie Treaty promises Sioux that they can keep their land in Dakota Territory
1869 transcontinental railway is completed
1876 Alexander Graham Bell invents the telephone
1876 Colorado becomes a state
1877 Chief Joseph of the Nez Perce surrenders and takes his people to a reservation
1879 Thomas Edison invents the electric light bulb
1881 Sitting Bull surrenders for his Sioux people
1886 Geronimo and the Apache surrender and move to a reservation.
1886 Statue of Liberty, a gift from France, is completed
1889 North Dakota, South Dakota, Washington and Montana become states
1889 former Native American land in Oklahoma is open for settlers
1890 Wyoming becomes a state
1890 soldiers kill hundreds of Native Americans at Wounded Knee Creek, South Dakota

Benjamin Harrison, 1833–1901, was the 23rd US president. He insisted that the American flag be flown above the White House, other government buildings and every school in the country.

James (Wild Bill) Hickok, 1837–1876, was sheriff of Ellis County, Kansas, and marshall of Abilene, Kansas, during the frontier days. He also was a Union spy during the Civil War, an army scout on the frontier, and a gambler.

Jesse James, 1847–1882, led a gang of bank and train robbers in Missouri and other states.

Andrew Johnson, 1808–1875, was the 17th US president. He was impeached by the House of Representatives. Many disapproved of his generosity to the South after the Civil War. The Senate voted to keep him in office.

Chief Joseph, 1840–1904, was a leader of the Nez Perce Native Americans. He tried to gain better treatment for his people, even by travelling to Washington and meeting with President Hayes.

Abraham Lincoln, 1809–1865, was the 16th US president. In 1863, he moved to end slavery with the Emancipation Proclamation. During the Civil War, his main goal was to preserve the Union.

Annie Oakley, 1860–1926, was born Phoebe Ann Moses in Ohio. She became a sharpshooter at the age of 8. In 1876, she changed her name and joined shooting contests.

Red Cloud, 1822–1909, was a warrior and a chief of the Oglala band of the Lakota Sioux. When settlers came on the Bozeman Trail to his territory in Wyoming, Red Cloud led successful attacks for two years. This was called Red Cloud's War.

Sitting Bull, 1831–1890, was a famous medicine man and spiritual leader of the Hunkpapa band of the Lakota Sioux.

Belle Starr, 1848–1889, was born Myra Maybelle Shirley. She was known as one of the few female outlaws in the US.

US presidents from 1840 to 1890

Martin Van Buren 1837–1841
William H. Harrison 1841
John Tyler 1841–1845
James Knox Polk 1845–1849
Zachary Taylor 1849–1850
Millard Fillmore 1850–1853
Franklin Pierce 1853–1857
James Buchanan 1857–1861
Abraham Lincoln 1861–1865
Andrew Johnson 1865–1869
Ulysses S. Grant 1869–1877
Rutherford B. Hayes 1877–1881
James A. Garfield 1881–1881
Chester A. Arthur 1881–1885
Grover Cleveland 1885–1889
Benjamin Harrison 1889–1893

SITTING BULL

1831 Sitting Bull is born
1867 Sitting Bull becomes a chief of the Hunkpapa Sioux
1868 after refusing to sign the Fort Laramie Treaty, Sitting Bull leads his people to the Black Hills of Dakota Territory
1874 gold is discovered in the Black Hills
1874 Sitting Bull refuses to sell the Black Hills to the US government
1876 Sitting Bull participates in the Sun Dance
1876 Sioux defeat Lieutenant Colonel George Custer at Little Bighorn River
1876 Sitting Bull leads his people to Canada
1878 by now, Sitting Bull has two wives and many children and grandchildren
1881 Sitting Bull surrenders and is arrested
1885 Sitting Bull joins Buffalo Bill's Wild West Show
1888 Sitting Bull is living with his people at Standing Rock Reservation in South Dakota
1889 the Sioux begin the Ghost Dance
1890 Sitting Bull is shot and killed

THE REST OF NORTH AND SOUTH AMERICA

1841 The Act of Union joins Upper and Lower Canada into the British Province of Canada
1846–1848 US–Mexican War. Mexico loses California, Arizona, New Mexico, Utah and Colorado
1864 Paraguay fights a major war with neighbouring countries
1867 Canada granted self-government by Britain
1868–1878 Cuba loses war of independence against Spain
1877 rise of dictator Porfirio Diaz in Mexico. He stays in power until 1911
1879 Chile at war with Bolivia (until 1883) and with Peru (until 1884). Chile victorious in both wars and gains much land
1880 start of the construction of the Panama Canal linking the Atlantic and Pacific Oceans

THE REST OF THE WORLD

1842 China hands over Hong Kong to Britain
1845 potato famine in Ireland
1848 revolutions in Italy, France, Austria and Germany
1850 Australia granted self-government by Britain
1854 US forces Japan to open its ports to Western trade
1854–1856 Crimean War – France and Britain help Turkey against Russia
1863 start of French empire in Indo-China
1869 Suez Canal is opened
1870 Franco–Prussian War: France defeated
1871 start of the German empire
1885 first motor car, in Germany
1887 Queen Victoria of Britain made Empress of India

GLOSSARY

agency office where services are provided, such as the office of an agent on a Native American reservation

agent person who takes care of things for other people, such as the person in charge of running each Native American reservation

amendment changes in a document, such as the US Constitution

boarding school school where students live during the school year

brand burned mark on an animal skin to show ownership

cattle drive long journey to walk cows, bulls and other cattle from a ranch to a town where they are loaded onto trains

Civil War war between people within a country; in the United States, fighting between northern and southern states from 1861 to 1865

claim to say that an area of land or an object belongs to you

Congress part of the US government that makes laws

deputy someone who has power to act for someone else, such as a sheriff's deputy

frontier land between a settled area and wilderness

Great Plains land between the Mississippi River and the Rocky Mountains

House of Representatives branch of US government that makes laws; part of Congress

illegal against the law

immigrant someone who moves from another country

jury group of people at a trial who listen to facts and decide if a person is guilty

lasso rope with a large loop that is thrown over an animal to catch it. The loop tightens as the rope is pulled.

marshall the law officer in charge of a town

peace-pipe in Native American tradition, a pipe that is smoked when people make an agreement

plains wide area of flat or gently rolling land

prairie wide area of flat or gently rolling land, such as the eastern part of the Great Plains

rancher someone who owns a large farm for cattle, horses or sheep – the farm is also called a ranch

reservation area of land set aside by the government for a special purpose, such as a place for Native Americans to live

saloon place where alcoholic drinks are sold

settler person who makes a home in a new place

sheriff law officer in charge of a county

slave person who is owned by another person and is usually made to work for that person

Supreme Court the highest court of law and order in the United States

surrender to give up or admit that you cannot win a battle

teepee tent-like shelter made of animal skins (also spelled tipi or tepee)

telegraph device for sending messages over long distances through codes of electric signals sent by wire

territory in the US, an area of land that is not yet a state

transcontinental crossing a continent such as the United States

treaty written agreement, usually to prevent or end a war

tribe group of people who share an area of land, language, customs and laws. Each tribe may be divided into a number of bands, or small groups, each with its own chiefs. A band may have one chief in charge of warriors in battle and a different chief in times of peace.

wagon train group of covered wagons that travelled to the West together

MORE BOOKS TO READ

Daily Life in a Plains Indian Village 1868,
Michael Bad Hand Terry, Heinemann.

Native American Stories. Robert Hull, Wayland.

The Indians of North America. F. Reynoldson,
and P. Shuter, Heinemann.

The Peoples of North America. C. Hatt, Evans.

PLACES TO VISIT

The British Museum
Ethnography Department
(formerly the separate Museum of Mankind)
Great Russell Street
London WC1B 3DG
Tel: 020 7636 1555

Horniman Museum,
London Road
London SE23 3PQ
Tel 020 8699 2339

The Pitt Rivers Museum
Parks Road
Oxford, OX1 3PP
Tel: 01865 270949

INDEX

INDEX